Eddy the Whirlpool

No matter how old we are, we always remain children of the universe

Eddy the Whirlpool

Gijs Hubben & Dalia Awad

THIS IS IT

FOREWORD

As we know, children are naturally close to their true being. This makes them especially open to the perennial understanding lying at the heart of all the great religious and spiritual traditions: that beneath our whirling thoughts and emotions we can find unshakeable peace and happiness. The children of today will also be running the world in thirty years! With this in mind, I'd like to warmly recommend Gijs Hubben's charming tale about the adventures of Eddy the Whirlpool. It unveils two timeless truths: that reality is a single, infinite and indivisible whole; and that happiness can be found in the understanding that we essentially are that reality. This is the simple joy of being.

RUPERT SPIRA

One day in the stream, a little whirlpool appeared. His friends called him Eddy. He looked around and saw other whirlpools like him, but mostly bigger.

Sometimes little Eddy wondered where he had come from, but he couldn't remember.

Eddy also didn't know where exactly he started or ended, but it didn't matter. He wasn't thinking about himself much.

He had so much fun being a whirlpool, just going round and round, playing with the water.

Then one day, while playing and spinning, Eddy saw one of the bigger whirlpools swallow a smaller one.

"What just happened?" he asked a friendly and slightly bigger whirlpool.

"Well, you're a small whirlpool, Eddy. If you don't grow big and strong, you'll get swallowed by one of those big guys, too."

"And then?"

"Then you're gone, buddy! It's game over."

Eddy was shocked, and started doing a lot of thinking.

After a while, he asked his older friend, "So how do I become a big whirlpool?"

"Well," his friend said, "you swallow smaller whirlpools."

This made Eddy very upset.

"Really? Swallow other whirlpools! Can that be right?"

But he didn't want to get swallowed and disappear. So he thought hard and long.

And then it came to him: he was going to be the biggest whirlpool of them all. Too big to be swallowed by anyone else.

So Eddy started looking around for smaller whirlpools that were just playing and not paying attention…

A long time passed and little Eddy became big Ed.

And Ed, who was now the biggest whirlpool in the stream, was in a pensive mood.

“I don’t feel very happy today,” he thought, “even though I’m bigger than everyone else.”

He noticed a few little whirlpools flow by, but he didn’t bother chasing them. He was so big now, catching them didn’t matter anymore.

As he watched the little whirlpools play and spin, he suddenly remembered how much he used to love doing that, too.

He felt a strange mix of joy and sadness as he remembered little Eddy. The sounds and feelings of his childhood came back to him, and tears welled up in his eyes.

But then he thought, “No! That was so dangerous and irresponsible back then. I could have been swallowed so easily. What a careless little whirlpool I used to be. Good thing I know better now.”

Many more seasons passed, and one day Ed noticed that he had slowed down a little. He was shocked and checked again. Yes, it was true! "Oh my," he thought, "I am spinning more slowly than before. And I've shrunk, too!"

Shocked and confused, he swirled over to his old friend, who had also become a huge whirlpool. Since neither of them was big enough to swallow the other, he was still a safe friend.

"I've shrunk today!" he said to his friend. "Can you believe it?"

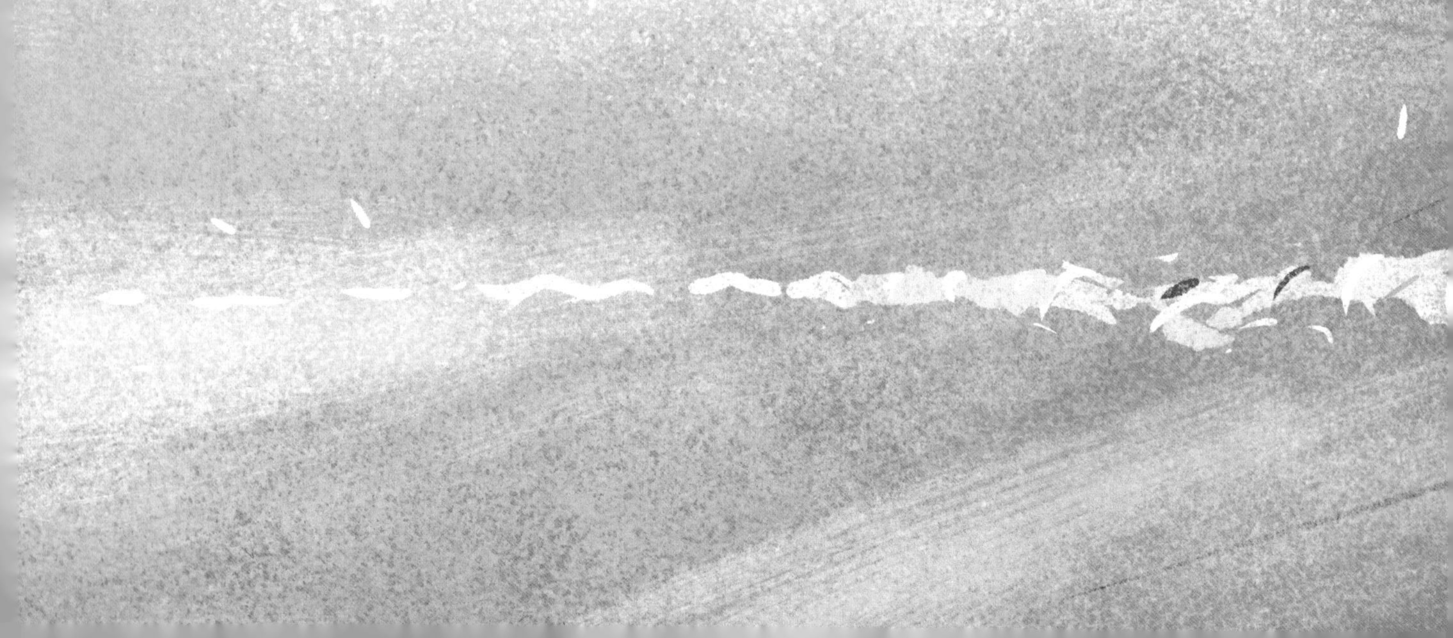

“Yes, of course,” his friend replied without paying much attention. “All whirlpools slow down and shrink someday. It’s the way of the stream.”

“The way of the what?” yelled big Ed, panicking. “Really? And then what happens?”

“Well, then it’s game over, buddy. You disappear.”

"But what's the point of getting large and strong, and working so hard chasing and swallowing other whirlpools, if we just disappear anyway?" By now Ed was very angry with his friend.

"Do you know how much work that is? And it's no fun at all!" he yelled.

Frustrated and disillusioned, he whirled away to a corner of the stream to be miserable by himself.

"Life sucks," he thought. "There's no point to any of it."

As if to make things deliberately worse for Ed, two young whirlpools flowed by, laughing and having fun bumping into each other. "Such nonsense," he thought.

Exhausted, he fell into a deep sleep and had a dream.

He dreamt of water.
Of endless, still water,
without any whirlpools or ripples.
There was just water
in all directions,
as far as he could see.

When he woke up, he noticed a peculiar whirlpool whirling by, one he'd seen before but never paid much attention to.

There was something different about him. Unlike other grown-up whirlpools, this one was flowing happily and didn't seem to have a care in the world.

"Hmm," Ed thought, "maybe that whirlpool knows something I don't..."

"Hello," he said, "I'm Ed. What's your name?"

"I'm Rupert," the happy whirlpool replied.

"How can you be so happy and carefree?" Ed asked.

"Don't you think it sucks being a whirlpool? It's so pointless."

"Well, yes, of course it sucks being a whirlpool," Rupert answered, "but I'm not a whirlpool. Bye!"

"Rupert! Wait! Wait! What do you mean you're not a whirlpool?"

"I mean I'm not a whirlpool," Rupert said.

"Huh?" said Ed. "What are you, then?"

"Water, of course!" Rupert said, "just like you. Bye!"

And off he whirled into the current, leaving big Ed behind in confusion.

"Like me?" Ed was so stunned that for a brief moment he forgot to keep spinning…

And then suddenly,
Rupert's words sank in.

"I am water!" he said. "I was never really a whirlpool! That's why I never knew where I came from, because I didn't come from anywhere!"

And in a flash Ed realised that if one day he stopped spinning, he wouldn't go anywhere.

"I am always here," he said to himself with a smile.

"I only started spinning because it was so much fun! I just love spinning! How could I have forgotten…"

And on went the water,

spinning some more,

enjoying itself.

Just spinning

for the sake of spinning,

happily ever after.

THIS IS IT

Eddy the Whirlpool

First published in 2024 by This Is It Media

www.thisisit.org

To request permissions or order copies, contact the publisher at publications@thisisit.org

ISBN 978–3–911268–01–1

Text by Gijs Hubben

Illustrations by Dalia Awad

Book design by Rob Bowden

Many currents flowed together to form this book, and like everything else in this universe, it's quite impossible to say where it came from! I would like to thank the following: Rupert, Kyra and the community for their support and encouragement; Dalia for her heartwarming artwork; Rob for his design; and Simone for her loving support and ideas. And thank you, Antoon and Lukas, my little whirlpools, for reminding me of my inner child, to whom this book is dedicated.

GIJS HUBBEN

When Gijs was seven years old, he invented a machine that makes breakfast. Curious about everything, Gijs went on to invent more things in the world of computers. After a long and busy journey, he found out that what he loves doing most is writing books for children and sailing on his boat. Gijs is from the Netherlands and lives in Germany with his wife and two sons.

www.thisisit.org

DALIA AWAD

Dalia is from Egypt and loves telling stories with her colourful art. At age four, her parents introduced her to the world of art, and she hasn't stopped doodling since. She enjoys playing with her cats and travelling to discover new stories to draw. Besides illustrating children's books, she also organises art workshops for children.

www.daliaawad.com

If you enjoyed our book, please support us with a review. Thank you!

Printed in Great Britain
by Amazon

45096170R00021